Indiana Wildlife

Animals & Mammals

Billy Grinslott & Kinsey Marie Books

ISBN - 9781968228033

Chipmunks are found in many areas. Chipmunks are small members of the squirrel family. They like to eat nuts and seeds. Chipmunks are most active during the day, especially at dawn and dusk. They have pouches inside of their cheeks so they can carry food. They are very friendly and will take food from your hand. Chipmunks need about 15 hours of sleep per day. The smallest chipmunk species is Tamias minimus, which is found throughout North America.

There are many squirrels in the wild. You may see a red or gray squirrel. The most popular is the gray squirrel. Squirrels are very acrobatic and can climb trees. Their favorite food is acorns. Squirrels hide their food in many small stashes and can find more than 90% of them later. Squirrels are fast and can run up a tree at 12 miles per hour. Newborn squirrels are blind, deaf, and hairless, and rely on their mother until they mature.

Flying Squirrels don't fly like birds. They don't have wings. They have skin that is attached to their legs. When they jump from a tree, they spread their legs out and glide through the air. Most glides are 30 feet from tree to tree. But they can glide up to 150 feet. They are primarily active at night and are social animals, often living in groups and sharing nests. They have large eyes for night vision, long whiskers for navigating in the dark, and a long, flattened tail for steering during glides.

Thirteen-lined ground squirrels, known for their 13 alternating light and dark stripes. They are true hibernators, entering their burrows in October and emerging in late March or early April, depending on soil temperature. They dig burrows that can be 15 to 20 feet long, often with multiple entrances. They use alarm calls and scent markings to communicate with other squirrels. They are social and like hanging out with other squirrels.

There are many types of rabbits in the wild. The most common is the cottontail. Rabbits are cute, friendly, and fun to watch. Many people have rabbits for pets. They have soft fluffy fur. They are called cottontails because they have a white fluffy tail that looks like a cotton ball.

The hare or jackrabbit is bigger than a rabbit with longer ears and legs. Their longs legs help them to run fast. They are agile and faster than most rabbits. Hares have excellent hearing and vision. Hares have large ears and eyes that are positioned on the sides of their head, giving them a wide field of vision. Hares can change color. Hares have the ability to change color depending on the season and their surroundings.

The American Mink lives across most of North America and is a cat sized. Mink are very skilled climbers and swimmers. They prefer to keep to themselves. They communicate using odors, visual signals, and other sounds. They purr when they're happy. Mink are agile swimmers, and they often dive to find food

The Stoat or ermine is part of the weasel family. Stoats can thrive in many climates and environments. They can live in most habitats if there's food and shelter. Stoats are opportunistic predators that hunt day and night. They have a strong sense of smell and can travel up to 1.5 miles in a few hours. Stoats are good at climbing trees. They can swim and dive underwater. Stoats can reach speeds of up to 20 miles an hour. In colder climates, stoats turn almost completely white, with just a black tip on their tail.

The least weasel is the smallest carnivore in North America, weighing only 1 to 2.5 ounces and measuring about 6 to 8 inches long. They can be found in a variety of habitats, including forests, woodlands, grasslands, and brushy fields. Their fur is soft and dense, with brown fur on top and white fur on the underside, including the chin and feet. Weasels are clever and highly intelligent.

Weasels are the smallest members of the meat-eating animals. Although small, they do not hibernate and are active all winter. Weasels in northern ranges turn white in the winter to camouflage in the snow. Weasels have long whiskers like cats, to help them feel things. They even have long whiskers on their elbows. When a weasel gets annoyed, it stomps its feet, just like humans do. Weasels are quick, agile, and alert animals. They are excellent climbers and swimmers.

Pocket gophers are burrowing rodents and are known for their digging activities and unique adaptations for underground life. They have very sharp claws for digging. They create complex underground tunnel systems. Their fur-lined cheek pouches, or pockets, are used to store and transport food, like roots, tubers, and grasses, back to their burrows. They can turn their cheek pouches inside out for grooming purposes. Their tails are highly sensitive and act as feelers to help them navigate the dark tunnels, even when backing up.

Groundhogs or woodchucks are the largest member of the squirrel family. Groundhogs get their name because of their big bodies, and they live underground. Groundhogs are skilled climbers and swimmers. Groundhogs are true hibernators, sleeping for up to six months. Groundhog Day is where Punxsutawney Phil predicts how long winter will last.

Beavers use their teeth to cut and knock down trees. They build dams with them to block water, so they have a place to live and swim. They also eat wood. Beavers can stay underwater for about 8 minutes. Beavers slap their tails on the water to indicate danger. Beavers are the largest rodents in North America.

Otters have the thickest fur of any animal. The otter is one of the few mammals that use tools, like rocks to break thing open. A group of otters resting together is called a raft.

Otters primarily rely on their sense of touch, whiskers, and forepaws, in murky waters to locate food. Otters have built in pouches of loose skin under their forearms to stash extra food when diving.

Muskrats are found in marshes, ponds, and streams with abundant aquatic vegetation. Muskrats have a scaly tail that acts as a rudder for swimming and helps them stay afloat. They primarily eat aquatic plants like cattails, sedges, and grasses, but also consume small animals like mussels, crayfish, and fish. They have a second set of lips that close behind their front incisors, enabling them to dive underwater, chew, and eat without swallowing water. They build lodges made of mud and vegetation, and also live in burrows along the banks of water sources.

Pee-ewe what is that stinky critter with the big bushy tail. It smells bad. Skunks are normally curious and friendly unless you scare them. If you scare them, they will flip their bushy tale at you and spray you with a smelly potion and it stinks. Skunks spray a smelly, sulfur-based liquid from their anal glands as a defense mechanism. The spray can cause eye irritation and temporary blindness. Skunks are highly adaptable and can thrive in many different environments. Skunks have strong forefeet and long claws for digging. Skunks live in dens.

Opossums or possums have strong tails and can hang from trees. One trick that a possum has, is when it feels danger is it will play dead. It will lay there and not move. Possums have white to gray face hair. Possums like to eat wood ticks. They are also immune to snakebites. Opossums are susceptible to frostbite because their hands and tails are not protected by fur. Opossums are marsupials, which means they have pouches for their young, like kangaroos and koalas.

Badgers have elongated heads, small ears, and black and white faces. Badgers live underground with other family members. Badgers are very social and live in groups. A badger den or sett can be centuries old and are used by many generations of badgers. Badgers are very territorial, it's best not to bother them is you see one. A group of badgers is called a cete, though they are often called clans. Badgers are largely nocturnal but reduce their activity during periods of cold weather.

Many Lemmings fur can change color with the seasons. Lemmings live in holes and tunnels that they dig in the ground. In winter they tunnel under the snow. Lemmings eat mosses, roots, and grasses. Lemmings are very small animals, usually, just three to six inches long. Their bodies are covered in thick fur and they don't hibernate during winter months.

Raccoons like to come out at night. Their eyes are made so they can see in the dark. Raccoons are highly intelligent and can solve problems. They can learn to open doors, trash cans, and other containers. They are called masked bandits because they like to raid and eat out of trash cans at night. Raccoons can survive in many environments.

Mallard ducks are by far the most recognizable and popular ducks in the world. They live in just about every area of North America. Their estimated population is around 19 million birds. The male is easily recognizable from its white neck ring and green neck and head. The female Mallard has between five to 14 light green eggs. Most ducks don't have green eggs, so this makes them unique. The male Mallard is called a drake and the female a hen. Female Mallards quack. Males don't quack, instead they produce deeper, raspier one- and two-note calls. They can also make rattling sounds by rubbing their bills against their flight feathers.

Canada Geese are the most sought after and abundant goose in North America. They live in many places. Canada geese can travel 1,500 miles in a day if the weather permits. Canada geese migrate every year. They fly in a V-formation, which allows them to travel long distances without stopping, as they can switch positions and conserve energy. Canada geese are known for their distinctive honk and are sometimes called Canadian honkers.

Ringed Neck Pheasants are one of the most sought-after birds in North America. They are found throughout most of Northern America and Canada. Ring-necked pheasants are not native to the US. Instead, they were brought here from Asia in the 1880's. South Dakota is one of the best places to find Pheasants.

The Wild Turkey is a large, bird that is native to North America. It is the heaviest bird in the United States and can weigh up to 24 pounds. Only male turkey's gobble. Wild turkeys can fly. Wild turkeys sleep in trees. Their heads can change colors. You can tell a turkey's emotions by the color of their heads. Colors can change from red to blue to white, depending on how excited or calm they are. You can find wild turkeys in just about every state in America.

Grouse, particularly ruffed grouse, are interesting birds known for their unique drumming displays. They flap or rotate their wings, and it sounds like drums. Grouse range in size from the small white-tailed ptarmigan at 13 inches long to the sage grouse at 30 inches long.

The bobwhite quail has the largest range of any game bird in America. Bobwhite quail are the most common species of quail, the bobwhite is often referred to as the number one game bird of the eastern and southern United States. Bobwhite quail are known for their explosive flight, and social behavior in groups called coveys.

Mourning Doves are unable to sweat, to stay cool during hot weather, they pant just like dog do. Mourning doves eat and collect seeds in their crop, which is an enlarged part of their esophagus. Then they digest them later. It's estimated that there are more than 100 million mourning doves in the US. With the southern states having the biggest population.

The national bird of the United States is the Bald Eagle. Bald eagles are large birds, with females up to 43 inches long and weighing up to 13 pounds. Their wingspan can be up to 7 feet wide. Bald eagles build the largest nests of any bird, up to 13 feet wide and weighing more than half a ton. Bald eagles aren't actually bald. The name bald eagle comes from the old English word piebald bird, which meant white-headed bird. Bald eagles have the best eyesight of any bird. A bald eagle can see up to three miles away, which is about four to five times farther than a human. They can also see small details like an ant on the ground from great distances.

Armadillos are known for their unique armor-like shells. Armadillos are the only living mammals with a hard shell, made of true bone and consisting of bands of plates connected by flexible skin. When threatened they can roll up into a ball and their shell protects them. Armadillos are primarily nocturnal animals, spending their days in burrows and emerging at night to forage for food. They are excellent diggers, using their strong claws and legs to burrow into the ground and forage for food, which primarily consists of insects and grubs. They also like to eat ant and termites.

Yes, there are feral hogs, often called wild boars or wild pigs, in Indiana. They are an invasive species found in numerous counties, primarily in the southern third of the state. Feral hogs are also known as wild boars. Feral hogs are known for their high reproductive rates and their tendency to root up the ground, which can lead to habitat destruction. They are highly intelligent, social animals with a keen sense of smell and a surprisingly good memory. Wild pigs can be found in various habitats, including forests, grasslands, and agricultural areas.

Bobcats are named for their short, bobbed tails with white tips. They have similar markings to lynxes but are much smaller. Bobcats live in a variety of habitats. Bobcats are skilled at leaping and can run up to 30 miles per hour.

Gray fox prefers to live in rocky canyons and ridges but can also be found in wooded areas and open fields. They have strong, hooked claws that enable them to climb trees. Which is abnormal for a dog species. Gray foxes are not observed as frequently as red foxes due to their reclusive nature and more nocturnal habits.

Red foxes have excellent hearing, allowing them to hear rodents digging underground from miles away. When afraid, red foxes grin or look like they are smiling. Red foxes front paws have five toes, while their hind feet only have four. Foxes dig underground dens where they raise their kits and hide from predators. A group of foxes is called a skulk or a leash. Babys are called kits and females are called vixens.

The coyote is bigger than a fox weighing between 20 and 45 pounds. Eastern coyotes are part wolf. Coyotes are great for pest control. They like to eat mice and rats. They can adapt and live almost anywhere, even in the city. Coyotes are very smart and have been observed learning and following traffic signals in some cities. They have a yip type of call when they communicate with each other. Coyotes are found in all the United States, except Hawaii.

Black bears are the smallest members of the bear family in North America. Black Bears love to eat sweet things like berries, fruits, and vegetables. They are good climbers and fast runners. They are excellent swimmers and can paddle at least a mile and a half in freshwater. They usually sleep for long periods of time and hibernate during the winter. They typically try to stay away from people unless they find food in the area.

The whitetail deer is the most popular deer in North America. Whitetail deer have good eyesight and hearing. They can detect small sounds from a quarter of a mile away. Only male deer grow antlers, which are shed each year. Whitetail deer are good swimmers and will use large streams and lakes to escape predators. A young deer is called a fawn, a male is a buck, and a female is called a doe. They are the most common deer species and live everywhere in North America.

The North American Bison and Buffalo are sometimes confused as the same animal, but they are not. Bison have long hair on their backs, front, and a long beard. Bison are bigger than buffalo. They are the largest mammal in North America and weigh up to 2,000 pounds. Bison can run up to 35 miles per hour. They can jump 6 feet vertically and more than 7 feet horizontally. Bison calves are nicknamed red dogs, because of their orange-red color at birth.

Fun Facts about Indiana Animals

1 – Whitetail deer were once nearly extirpated in Indiana. They were re-introduced and are now very abundant throughout the state.

2 - The largest mammal in Indiana is the bison or buffalo. Bison can be found at Kankakee Sands in Northwest Indiana, Wild Winds Buffalo Preserve in Steuben County, Broken Wagon Bison in Hobart.

3 - Indiana is home to a diverse array of animal life, including at least 52 species of mammals and over 250 species of birds.

4 - The smallest mammal in Indiana is the American Pygmy Shrew. This tiny mammal weighs only about two grams, less than a dime.

5 - The largest native cat species currently found in Indiana is the bobcat. Cougars used to live in Indiana, but not any longer.

6 – The Coyote is the largest wild dog in Indiana. They are very adaptive and can live almost everywhere including in the cities.

7 – The black bear is the only species of bear in Indiana. They were almost extirpated but have made a comeback in recent years.

Author Page

Billy Grinslott & Kinsey Marie Books

ISBN – 9781968228033

Thanks

9781968228033